398.2 Blumberg, Rhoda
BLU
        The truth about
        dragons

DATE			

THE TRUTH ABOUT DRAGONS

by

Rhoda Blumberg

THE TRUTH ABOUT DRAGONS

illustrated by

Murray Tinkelman

FOUR WINDS PRESS   NEW YORK

LIBRARY OF CONGRESS CATALOGING IN PUBLICATION DATA

Blumberg, Rhoda.
The truth about dragons.

Bibliography: p.
SUMMARY: Discusses the physical appearance, size,
habitat, diet, mating, habits, and enemies of western and
eastern dragons and cures and charms concerning them.
1. Dragons — Juvenile literature. [1. Dragons]
I. Tinkelman, Murray. II. Title.
GR830.D7B57   398.2'454   79-19589
ISBN 0-590-07570-5

Published by Four Winds Press
A division of Scholastic Magazines, Inc., New York, N.Y.
Text copyright © 1980 by Rhoda Blumberg
Illustrations copyright © 1980 by Murray Tinkelman
All rights reserved
Printed in the United States of America
Library of Congress Catalog Card Number: 79-19589
1   2   3   4   5   84   83   82   81   80

This book is for my grandson, Daniel.

CONTENTS

INTRODUCTION

Nobody knows just when our ancestors first saw dragons. It was long, long ago, probably before books were written. We know from ancient records that people in countries all over the world have been seeing dragons for at least 5,000 years.

Experts classify dragons as members of the Monster family. There are two distinct kinds, or species: Western Dragons, and Eastern Dragons. They must be studied separately, because they differ from each other in personality traits and in habits. This book is therefore divided into two parts.

Part I will acquaint you with Western Dragons, who are usually ugly, vicious, and extremely dangerous. They have always been hated and feared, for good reasons: they steal jewels and money, destroy property, and kill people. Western Dragons have been sighted in Europe, Africa, and western Asia.

After learning about their mean and evil ways, read Part II, and compare them with the Eastern Dragons, who are beautiful, gentle, and friendly. They have always been loved and revered, for they can be kind and helpful.

Meeting a Western Dragon can be a terrifying experience, while encountering an Eastern Dragon is usually an honor and a pleasure.

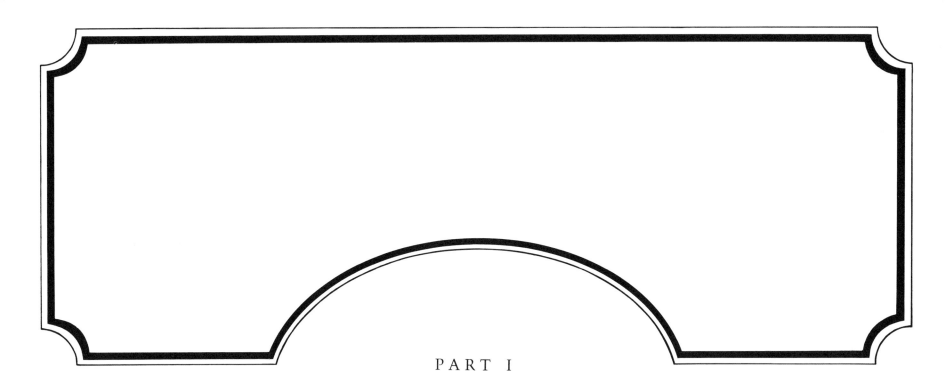

PART I

WESTERN DRAGONS

WESTERN DRAGONS

From ancient reports, it is clear that Western Dragons are the most terrible and terrifying of all animals. They spread disease, kill crops, and enjoy attacking and eating people. First confined to Africa and the ancient countries of Persia and Babylonia, these dangerous beasts found their way to Europe. They flew, slithered, and swam, invading Europe from Sicily to Scandinavia.

During the Middle Ages, when people suffered from poverty and plagues, dragons added to their miseries. The monsters roamed the countryside, especially at night. Anything from soured milk to sudden sickness was proof that they lurked nearby.

People knew that Western Dragons could be like poison tanks. Not only their fangs, but their bodies are filled with venom. The poison of some dragons is so strong that should a man on horseback stab the monster with a spear, the venom will travel up the spear, destroying horse and rider.

When dragons fly through the air their jaws and skins drip poisons that cause everything from pimples to plagues. People often starved because a dragon's sweat and saliva had killed crops.

Fortunately, the number of dragon reports declined as centuries passed. Father Kircher, a seventeenth-century expert in earth sciences, explained that most dragons are hiding underground. In his book *The Subterranean World*, he wrote that the reptiles are rarely seen because they prefer to remain in caves and in holes beneath the earth's surface. Few dragons come out in the open. Some have lost their way. Others can't return to their lairs because an earthquake or landslide has blocked their passage home. According to Father Kircher, most of the world's dragon population remains unseen beneath our feet.

Physical Appearance

The Historie of Serpents, by Edward Topsell, published in 1608, describes three basic kinds of dragons: "There be some Dragons which have wings and no feet, some again have both feet and wings, and some neither feet nor wings." Those without feet and wings don't look like ordinary snakes because they have crests on their heads and yellow beards on their chins.

The most common variety of dragons has wings and two or four feet. It is a heavy reptile with bulging eyes, batlike wings, and huge jaws equipped with razor-sharp teeth. Its body is covered with rough scales, and its long pointed tail has poisonous spikes that are as sharp as daggers. Its feet have sharp curved claws for clutching victims. It has poison fangs, a forked tongue, and a stinking breath that could choke a person to death. Because its insides burn like a furnace, it spits fire, and smoke streams out of its nostrils.

The ancient Greeks were horrified by hydras, sea dragons with nine or more heads. As centuries passed, only seven-headed hydras were seen. The seventeenth-century naturalist Edward Topsell included a picture of a hydra in *The Historie of Serpents.* He wrote that a hydra, shipped from Venice to Turkey in 1530, was exhibited in public before being presented to the King of France.

Dragons with horses' heads and snakes' bodies, and with fishes' fins and crocodiles' bodies have long scared seafarers. Norwegian sailors used to throw castor oil overboard, hoping the nasty tasting stuff would keep such monsters away. They also carved their ships to look like fierce dragons, ready to devour any beast that swam close. Interestingly enough, sea dragons have been reported during the twentieth century.

Dragons are yellow, black, silver, gray, slimy green, or bloodred. A few rare types are multicolored.

Dragons hiss, grunt, and roar. When injured they howl and scream.

Size

Although most Western Dragons are fifteen to twenty feet long — the size of large crocodiles — a few varieties are less than four feet long when full-grown.

Supersized dragons have always been seen more frequently than tiny terrors. One African reptile attacked the Roman army of General Regulus. According to the Roman historian Livy, "After many of the soldiers had been seized in [the dragon's] mouth, and many more crushed by the folds of its tail, its hide being too thick for javelins and darts, the dragon was at last attacked by military engines and crushed by repeated blows from heavy stones."

This dragon was a midget compared with another African monster described by the geographer Iphicrates. His dragon had grass growing on its back. It was so big that Iphicrates said people mistook it for a meadow.

The smallest and most fearsome of all dragons was the basilisk. This mini-monster, ranging in size from six inches to two feet, had the head of a rooster, the warts of a toad, and the body of a snake. It hid in wells and in cellars. The basilisk's death-ray eyes killed with a look. Anyone it glared at dropped dead. Once common in Europe, basilisks were killed off by clever people who used mirrors as shields. The monsters died of fright when they saw their own horrid reflections.

Habitat

Most dragons live in caves above or underground, but they also make themselves at home in any field. The smallest varieties live almost everywhere, in holes in the ground, in trees, tombs, tunnels, wells, and cellars.

Dragons over one hundred feet long have been discovered on mountaintops. These are golden in color, with arched eyebrows and long, flowing beards. They bed down on top of gold mines or make their dens in mountain caves.

Black dragons as big as elephants have homes hidden in marshes. They are sluggish monsters, able to hunt only those animals and people who come near their mud-mound dwellings. Survival is a struggle, especially because the mountain dragons come down to steal their food.

Silver-colored dragons live in rivers. Other water dwellers live in the ocean. And there are fishlike reptiles that shine in the night, startling people living near large European and African lakes.

Social Order

Western Dragons are property owners. Each male claims a territory, which he rules as his private kingdom. He welcomes female dragons, but treats males as enemies. When a male offspring grows up, or another male comes by, there's a dragged-out dragon fight. The loser leaves, his pride and his hide wounded. He is an outcast, forced to wander until he finds his own territory to terrorize.

Diet

Dragons enjoy milk, maidens, cakes, birds, oxen, deer, and elephants' blood.

Milk is their favorite drink. It makes them sleepy and too drunk to harm anyone. Egyptians, Greeks, and Romans used to leave milk at the entrances to dragon caves. They also left honey cakes to satisfy the beast's sweet tooth. European housekeepers used to leave milk outside their homes for stray, thirsty dragons. They didn't want to invite the monsters over for a visit, but they hoped that milk would make the creatures so drowsy that they wouldn't eat people. Unmarried daughters were in the gravest danger, for sweet, tender maidens are a tasty dish.

When dragons hunger for a snack, they open their jaws, lift their heads, and inhale deeply. The force of their breath creates a draft. Birds flying overhead are sucked into their mouths and down their throats.

There were reports of a mammoth man-eater in Africa that would eat twice as fast as any other dragon, because it had two heads. This double-header was finally killed by lightning. What a stroke of luck!

Although their teeth are as sharp as steak knives, some full-grown dragons gulp down victims whole, without biting or chewing. After swallowing an ox or a deer they twist themselves around trees, crushing the animals they have eaten.

Old nature books claimed that dragons swallow elephants whole, and then cough up the bones. This has been questioned by experts who insist that dragons only like elephants' blood. They wait in trees until elephants pass below, then pounce upon the big gray beasts. Coiling themselves around the elephants' bodies, and biting the tips of the ears, they suck the elephants dry. The elephants become empty bags of skin and bones. The foolhardy dragons keep drinking until they blow up like balloons. When the elephants fall down dead, the dragons wrapped around them are crushed to death.

Some African dragons in search of food used to cross the Red Sea to Arabia. Four or five twisted themselves together into a floating raft. The dragons' heads were held high above the water, acting as sails, as the beasts rode the waves. Once ashore, they headed for apple orchards and feasted until their bellies ached. Then they grazed for lettuce, their remedy for instant relief from indigestion.

Having Babies

Winged dragons fly high and mate in midair, usually during a heat wave. Some people believe that the heat wave is caused by the fire-breathing monsters when they get together above the clouds for their mating season.

Because dragons' dens are hidden in remote places, and because these are very dangerous to enter, no one has been able to observe the Western Dragon's family structure. And although books tell us many facts about dragons, they usually refer to male dragons, as though females weren't important. Perhaps the females were forced to remain hidden, busy bearing and rearing babies.

Small lizards and salamanders have been mistaken for baby dragons. Specimens of small, stuffed reptiles were exhibited as dragons in European museums until the 1930s. These are fakes. Some are lizards with bats' wings glued on. Other fakes are made of ocean skates and rays cut and shaped to look like dragons. The most common display is a dried four-inch lizard from Malaysia, whose ribs stick out like wings. Many of these fakes are now owned by private collectors who show them off as real baby dragons.

Hoarding Treasure

Western Dragons are miserable misers. Although they haven't any real use for money and jewels, they collect heaps of gold and gems. And they try to kill anyone coming near their hoard.

Miser dragons have bloodshot eyes. That's because they are always on the lookout for people who try to steal their treasures. They even sleep with their eyes open. Their eyes are red from the strain of never closing them, and from the glare of glittering gold and sparkling jewels.

Gold is a magnet that attracts dragons. The Roman writer Pliny relates that hunters baited a dragon by hanging gold at the entrance to its cave. When the beast came out, the hunters played soft music to lull it to sleep. Then they cut off its head.

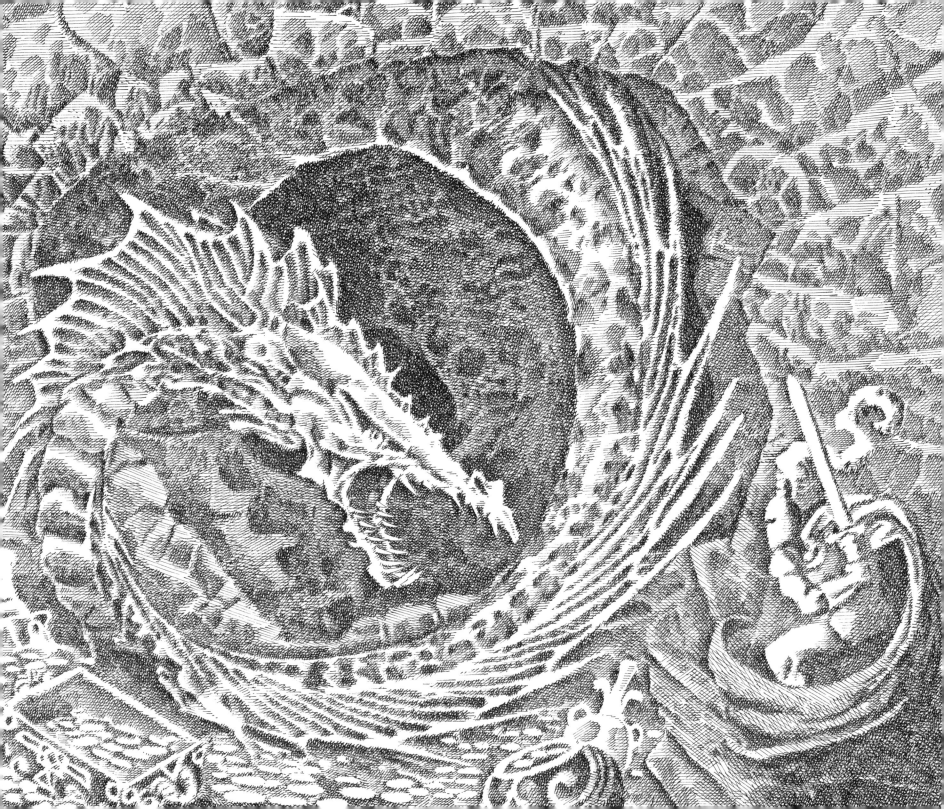

Enemies

Eagles and panthers hate dragons, for reasons no one can explain. Eagles swoop down and peck dragons to death. Panthers attract dragons with their sweet, perfumed breaths, then claw and kill them.

Men and women are the dragon's worst enemies. Because the monster was dangerous and destructive, it was accused of being the Devil in disguise. Thus, dragon slaying became a holy mission.

St. George is probably the most famous knight ever to kill a dragon. He stabbed the monster with his sword. Many saints didn't need swords. St. Martha, for example, just sprinkled a dragon with holy water, and led it out of town, using a silken cord as a leash. St. Marcell's dragon dropped dead merely by being tapped on the head with the Holy Cross, and St. Ammon destroyed his dragon by reciting a prayer.

In addition to saints, heroes of many lands were dragon slayers. Ragnar, King of Denmark, killed a dragon that had captured a beautiful maiden, then married the maiden. Siegfried, a German warrior, slew one that guarded treasure, then found a mound of gold. An unknown named John Smith rid Deerhurst, England, of a dragon that was gobbling people. He first fed the monster milk to make it sleepy, then stabbed it with his sword.

The island of Rhodes was saved from another people-eater by Theodore de Gozon, a young man from France. Theodore built and set up a paper dragon in his backyard. He trained his two dogs to attack the paper foe. Mounted on his father's horse, Theodore pretended to fight his homemade monster. He practiced with dummy dragons for two months before taking his animals and setting sail for Rhodes. When he found the real dragon, his dogs attacked, causing the beast to rear up and expose its breast. Theodore charged on horseback, and sank his sword into the dragon's heart. He earned the title, "Defender of Rhodes."

The last of the basilisks (see p. 9) was destroyed in Warsaw, Poland, in 1587. After two little girls and their nursemaid were found dead in a cellar, city officials concluded that a basilisk was probably the killer. John Faurer, a criminal doomed to be hanged, volunteered to encounter the monster. Outfitted in a leather suit covered with sewed-on mirrors, he shut his eyes, and descended the cellar stairs. Armed with an iron rake, he poked about until he stabbed a rubbery object. Then, with his eyes still closed, he groped his way up and out to the street. Upon examining the thing at the end of Faurer's rake, Warsaw's Chief Physician declared it to be a dead basilisk. As a reward for his bravery the criminal was set free.

Some heroic dragon slayers discovered that when they were splashed with the monster's blood, they could understand the language of birds and beasts. Others found that by bathing in dragon blood they became so thick-skinned that no sword could harm them.

Cures and Charms

There's a German saying, "A dragon can blow poison through stone walls, but not through knitted stockings." A few persons carried extra stockings to hold over their faces, in case they met a dragon. Most people used time-tested charms: salt and iron (also successful against witches and demons). They sprinkled salt around their houses, and nailed iron horseshoes over their doors. Burning bones and filth to make smelly smoke also drove dragons away.

Do you feel nervous about meeting an important person? Carry dragons' teeth, and even kings will be kind to you.

Do you have nightmares? Rub yourself with an ointment made from dried dragons' eyes and honey.

Are you worried about a lawsuit? Place the fat of a dragon's heart in the skin of a gazelle and tie it to your arm with deer muscle. You will win your case.

This advice comes from the thirty-seven volume *Natural History* by Pliny, a first-century Roman. By mentioning that some dragons have a precious jewel inside their heads, he gave dragon hunting a boost for at least 1500 years.

PART II

EASTERN DRAGONS

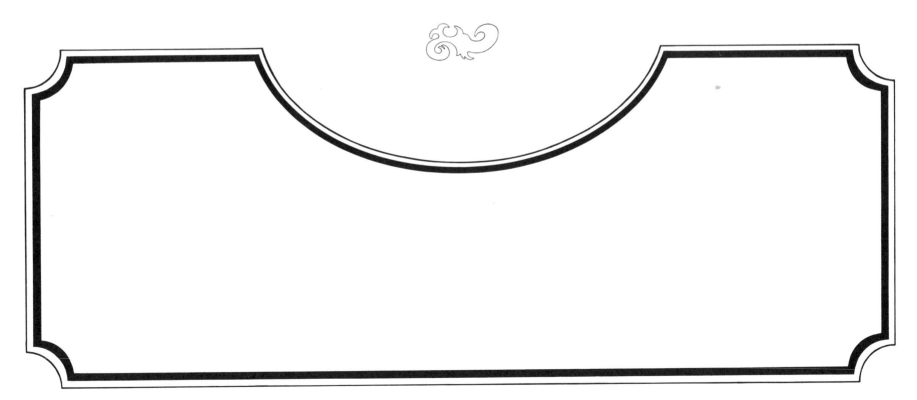

EASTERN DRAGONS

Unlike the ugly, nasty, Western types, most Eastern Dragons are beautiful, friendly, and wise. They are the angels of the Orient. Instead of being hated, they are loved and worshipped. Temples and shrines have been built to honor them, for they control the rain, rivers, lakes, and seas.

Many Chinese cities have pagodas where people used to burn incense and pray to dragons. The Black Dragon Pool Chapel, near Peking, was reserved for the Empress and her court. Special worship services took place there on the first and fifteenth of every month.

Dragon shrines and altars can still be seen in many parts of the Far East. They are usually along seashores and riverbanks, because most Eastern Dragons live in water. The Isle of the Temple, in Japan's Inland Sea, has become a famous stopover for pilgrims who meditate and pray to dragons.

Everything connected with Eastern Dragons is blessed. The Year of the Dragon, which takes place ever twelve years, is lucky. Present-day Oriental astrologers claim that children born during Dragon Years enjoy health, wealth, and long life. (1964 and 1976 were Dragon Years.)

Dragons are so wise that they have been royal advisors. A thirteenth-century Cambodian king spent his nights in a golden tower, where he consulted with the real ruler of the land — a nine-headed dragon.

Eastern Dragons are vain, even though they are wise. They are insulted when a ruler doesn't follow their advice, or when people don't honor their importance. Then, by thrashing about, dragons either stop making rain and cause water shortages, or they breathe black clouds that bring storms and floods. Small dragons do minor mischief, such as making roofs leak, or causing rice to be sticky.

People set off firecrackers and carry immense paper dragons in special parades. They also race dragon-shaped boats in water — all to please and appease their dragons.

Physical Appearance

The ancient sage Wang Fu described an Eastern Dragon: "Its head is like a camel's, its ears like a cow's, its neck like a snake's, its belly like a frog's, its scales like a carp's, its claws like an eagle's, and its paws like a tiger's." It has whiskers on the sides of its mouth and a bright pearl growing under its chin.

That's only one kind. Most Eastern Dragons have horns and whiskers, but their heads often resemble cows' or horses'. They never look like the horrible snake-dragons of the West. They rarely have wings, and they breathe clouds, not fire. Their voices sound like jingling coins, ringing bells, or clanging gongs.

Instead of wings, the dragon has a "poh shan," a growth on top of its head that pumps air in and out, lifting the creature high in the sky. Winds enable it to sail through the air. Some scholars claim that the pearl under its chin makes the dragon airborne, but how this works has never been explained.

There are odd-looking varieties. Horse-headed dragons have been showing up for at least 5,000 years. One specimen had wings at its side, and walked on top of the water. Another tossed its mane back and forth making noises that sounded like a flute.

Cow-heads are also common. A ten-footer, found lying on the banks of China's Yangtze River, was different from most because of its long, thick eyebrows. A Yellow River variety, seen on shore in the 1920s by a Chinese teacher, was bright blue, and as big as five cows. Both dragons crawled into the water as soon as it started to rain.

Size

Dragons are as small as silkworms and as large as mountains. Tiny ones may cluster under window ledges and on rooftops. It's possible to find them hiding in the seams of a robe.

There are almost as many Asiatic dragons as there are fish in the sea, and they come in all sizes.

Giant dragons are so big and powerful, they control the forces of nature. When they breathe, they make clouds; when they inhale water, they cause whirlpools. Underground dragons create hills by humping their backs.

Supersized Oriental dragons are miles long. They are the biggest, grandest, most powerful animals in the whole world.

Habitat

Many dragons are year-round sea dwellers.

Land and sky dragons that don't like cold weather spend their winters at the bottom of the ocean. Their marineland vacation ends in the spring when they surface, and either float up to the sky, or go ashore. Autumn frosts have them hurrying back to their underwater homes. Whenever dragons enter and leave the sea, they disturb the air and water causing floods and hurricanes.

Every pond, lake, river, and stream has its resident dragons. Although numerous, they are rarely seen, because they're so shy that they sink when anybody watches them.

Thousands of Eastern Dragons make their homes inside mountains and under the ground. They don't like to be disturbed, and they can become so bad tempered that experts in "feng shui" are consulted before anyone digs in the soil. Feng shui is the art of placing graves, homes, and buildings in locations that won't bother dragons. Experts have a mysterious instinct for sensing just where underground dragon paths lie, even though these are out of sight. The paths must never be touched.

Social Order

The dragon empire is ruled by Dragon Kings. The Celestial King keeps the sky from falling; the Spiritual King is in charge of wind and rain; the Earth King rules rivers and streams, and the King of Hidden Treasures guards the underground. Five Dragon Kings rule the oceans, dividing their territories into East, West, North, South, and Central Seas.

Cabinet ministers, department heads, and minor officials help run a well-organized dragon government.

Because people know about this government, they can write prayers on paper addressed to the proper officials. For example, they may write to the Dragon Minister of the Department of Sweet Waters asking for cleaner wells; or they may address the King of the Eastern Seas, begging for a calmer ocean. Whenever a dragon is out of sorts, housekeepers hang yellow papers with images of the offended dragon outside their homes.

Diet

Bamboo, milk and cream, the flesh of swallows, and arsenic are favorite foods. Although to people it's a deadly poison, arsenic merely makes dragons fat.

In 1611 B.C., the Emperor of China appointed the first Royal Dragon Feeder, whose duty was to throw food into sacred dragon ponds. Royal Dragon Feeder was an honored post for centuries.

The custom of feeding dragons was common throughout the Orient. According to the *Buddhist Records*, a dragon chapel on the banks of the Indus River had a copper vessel filled with cream for a white-eared river dragon.

As a rule, Eastern Dragons never eat people. But woe to anyone who dines on roasted swallows and rides in a boat. Dragons, detecting the scent of the digested birds, will overturn the boat and swallow the swallow-swallower.

Wise people never offer mong plants to dragons. Although mong is a delicious vegetable used in Oriental cooking, it makes dragons irritable. And when an Eastern Dragon is out of sorts, it can cause storms, floods, and earthquakes.

Having Babies

Eastern Dragons mate frequently. The female usually gives birth to nine at a time. Each baby differs. The first sounds like a bell, the second like a harp, the third is always thirsty, the fourth loves to climb, the fifth is a fighter, number six is a scholar, the seventh has keen hearing, the eighth just sits around, and the ninth is a weight lifter.

Images of these nine dragons decorate various objects. For example, the weight lifter is carved on the bottom of monuments; the fighter, on sword handles; the thirsty one is painted on drinking cups, and the scholar-dragon is printed on textbooks.

Some dragons lay eggs near mountain streams, and then desert them. The hen-sized eggs look like beautiful stones. They hatch when lightning splits them open. Then the infant dragon immediately floats to the sky.

A few dragons begin life as fish. Carp who sucessfully jump rapids and leap over waterfalls change into fish-dragons. A popular saying, "The carp has leaped through the dragon's gate," means success, especially for students who have passed their exams.

Male dragons sometimes mate with other kinds of animals. A dragon fathers an elephant when he mates with a pig, and he sires a racehorse, after mating with a mare.

The offspring of a dragon and a cow is a "kirin," shown here.

Both male and female dragons have mated with humans. Their descendants became great rulers. The Japanese Emperor Hirohito traced his ancestry back 125 generations to Princess Fruitful Jewel, daughter of a Dragon King of the Sea.

Emperors in many Asian countries claimed to have dragon ancestors. This made them so proud, that everything they used was decorated with dragons and described in terms of the dragon: dragon-throne, dragon-robe, dragon-bed, dragon-boat. Calling an emperor "dragon-face" was a supreme compliment.

People believed that rulers could change themselves into dragons. For hundreds of years, Japanese emperors sat concealed behind bamboo curtains whenever visitors came. Anyone who dared to peek was condemned to death.

Enjoying Treasure

Like dragons all over the world, Eastern Dragons love jewels and precious stones. They prefer jade, coral, and pearls to gold, silver, and diamonds.

Unlike their Western cousins, Eastern Dragons are not misers. They make use of their treasure, wearing jewelry and building undersea palaces of coral and pearls. And they are so generous that they give gifts of gems to people lucky enough to meet them.

Unfortunately, although typical Eastern Dragons are gentle and giving, there are exceptions. Japanese pearl divers fear shark-dragons, which threaten to attack them as they work. Shark-dragons also patrol wrecked ships.

Nagas, the many-headed dragon snakes of India and Southeast Asia, can be killers. Although some Nagas aren't dangerous, most of them can't be trusted. They can be as nasty as Western Dragons. Nagas love to wear jewels and build palaces of gems. They are as skillful at jewel-craft as their Chinese relatives.

Enemies

The centipede is the Eastern Dragon's one known enemy. Although only two inches long, it can destroy the biggest dragon by walking up its nose, into its head, and feasting on its brain.

Cures and Charms

Dragon blood, fat, brains, saliva, teeth, and horns are miracle medicines curing everything from measles to madness. Dragon bones are the best remedies, and also easiest to find.

Until 1927 entire villages in China supported themselves by digging and selling dragon bones. Visiting scientists from the American Museum of Natural History were very upset when they saw warehouses filled with the bones, because they claimed that these were fossils of prehistoric animals. They bought and shipped huge quantities to their museum in New York City, and presented some to a museum in Peking. Thereafter, selling dragon-bone medicine was forbidden. However, an undercover dragon-bone business continues to cater to customers all over the Orient.

Here is a handy list of other useful products:

Dragon whiskers: for keeping flies and mosquitoes away; also a boon to fishermen, because they attract fish when placed in a stream. The best quality whiskers are three feet long, and deep purple.

Dragon saliva: an excellent ink for marking jade and gold; a base for the finest perfume and incense. The saliva is found floating on the ocean's surface.

Dragon meat: reserved for royal kitchens. Emperor Hwo ordered soup made from a dragon that fell on his palace grounds during a storm. He and his ministers enjoyed the broth. Emperor Chao handed his chefs a tusked dragon which he caught while fishing in the Wei River. The dragon was delicious "brain food." After eating it, Emperor Chao was able to write brilliant essays.

Dragon paths are more important than dragon products. To assure good fortune, locate your home, your business, and the family burial plot near underground dragon paths. Feng shui experts can be hired to advise you. They own round wooden compasses that point to the paths and they sometimes taste the soil before deciding upon a lucky site. People swear by them, but in some cases they swear at them.

In 1976 feng shui advisors were blamed when water pipes burst and elevators broke in a Hong Kong skyscraper. But feng shui experts must have a good record, for they have customers all over the world.

Some people are guided by the stars, others by dragon paths.

BIBLIOGRAPHY

Aelian, Claudius. *Of the Nature of Animals.* London: Heinemann, 1958.

Binyon, Laurence. *The Flight of the Dragon.* London: John Murray, 1911.

Gosse, Philip. *The Romance of Natural History.* Philadelphia: J.B. Lippincott, 1970.

Gould, Charles. *Mythical Monsters.* London: W.H. Allen, 1886.

Hayes, L. Newton. *The Chinese Dragon.* Shanghai: Commercial Press, 1922.

Herodotus. *The Histories.* Baltimore: Penguin Books, 1954.

Ingersoll, Ernest. *Dragons and Dragon Lore.* New York: Payson & Clarke, 1928.

Kircher, Athanasius. *Mundus Subterraneus (The Subterranean World).* Amsterdam: Joannem Jansonnium à Waesberge, 1678.

Ley, Willy. *Dawn of Zoology.* Englewood Cliffs, N.J.: Prentice-Hall, 1968.

———. *Exotic Zoology.* New York: Viking Press, 1959.

———. *The Lungfish, the Dodo, and the Unicorn.* New York: Viking Press, 1948.

Lum, Peter. *Fabulous Beasts.* London: Thames & Hudson, 1952.

Minton, Sherman A., Jr. and Rutherford, Madge. *Giant Reptiles.* New York: Charles Scribner's Sons, 1973.

Pliny the Younger. *Natural History.* London: Heinemann, 1938.

Pontoppidan, Erik. *The Natural History of Norway.* London: Folio, 1755.

Topsell, Edward. *The Historie of Serpents.* London: E. Cotes, 1608.

Visser, M.W. *The Dragon in China and Japan.* Amsterdam: J. Mueller, 1913.

White, T.H. *The Bestiary.* New York: Capricorn Books, 1960.